The vehicle that firmly established Humber as a car manufacturer was the Humberette, of which several thousand were made between June 1903 and the autumn of 1905. This is an early model with 5 horsepower engine and wire wheels.

THE HUMBER

Nick Georgano

Shire Publications Ltd

CONTENTS

Printed in Great Britain by C. I. Thomas & Sons (Haverfordwest) Ltd, Press Buildings, Merlins Bridge, Haverfordwest, Dyfed SA61 1XF.

British Library Cataloguing in Publication Data: Georgano, G. N. (George Nicholas). The Humber. 1. Great Britain. Cars, history. I. Title. 629.2'272'09 ISBN 0-7478-0057-X.

Editorial consultant: Michael E. Ware, Curator of the National Motor Museum, Beaulieu.

ACKNOWLEDGEMENTS

All photographs were provided by the National Motor Museum, with the exception of the cover which is by the author, and those on pages 10 (above), 20 (top) and 24, which are acknowledged to the Peter Roberts Collection (c/o Neill Bruce), James Griffin and the Imperial War Museum respectively.

Cover: *A 1907 Coventry Humber 15 horsepower tourer made late in 1906 and owned by the Fattorini family.*

Below: *Humber was one of many British firms to make tricars, which became gradually more car-like. This is a 1905 Olympia Tricar De Luxe which had a seat for the driver and wheel steering, whereas earlier models had saddles and handlebars.*

The Humber Phaeton of 1899, which was offered with engines of 3, 3½, and 5 horsepower. Common to all models were a horizontal single-cylinder air-cooled engine ('fully exposed to all the winds that blow', said 'The Autocar') and belt final drive.

INTRODUCTION

During the last quarter of the nineteenth century the cycle industry experienced a tremendous boom all over Europe, and in Britain few companies enjoyed a higher reputation than Humber. Thomas Humber, born in Sheffield in 1841, began his working life as a blacksmith; in 1867 his employer, William Campion, brought back from Paris a Michaux velocipede. This was a simple bicycle with pedal acting directly on the front wheel. Humber built six copies for Campion and then began to make improvements of his own, including a more graceful frame and a larger front wheel. He went into business on his own and produced his first catalogue in 1873, gaining partners and increased capital over the next few years. The early works were at various addresses in Nottingham, but in 1878 Humber, Marriott and Cooper, as it was then, moved to new premises at Beeston, near Nottingham.

The early Humber bicycles were developments of the velocipede and had front wheels of increasing size, becoming the famous Ordinary, nicknamed 'penny farthing'. The front wheel ranged from 44 to 58 inches (112 to 147cm) in diameter, according to the leg length of the rider. Tricycles were made from 1878 and the new safety bicycle with chain drive to the rear wheel from 1887. In that year new factories were acquired in Wolverhampton and Coventry, and in the 1890s branches were set up in Paris and in Westboro, Massachusetts, in a factory later used for the manufacture of Locomobile steam cars. The cautious Thomas Humber left his company in 1892, but this enabled his successors to expand further, and by 1900 Humber Limited was one of the largest cycle firms in Britain.

3

CARS FROM COVENTRY AND BEESTON

Humber made several unsuccessful attempts at car manufacture before regular production was established. The first came in 1896 when the Coventry bicycle factory received a contract to make the French-designed Léon Bollée three-wheeler, a strange device with tandem seating for two and a 650 cc single-cylinder horizontal engine driving the rear wheel by belts. Ignition was by hot tube. The financier H. J. Lawson had paid the French inventor £20,000 for the British manufacturing rights, but his, and Humber's, hopes were dashed when the factory burnt to the ground on 17th July 1896, leaving no trace of the drawings or of the Bollée car itself. However, a second car and set of drawings were obtained from France, and Humber found temporary premises in the Motor Mills at Coventry, which were owned by the Great Horseless Carriage Company, and where Daimler and MMC cars were built from 1897 onwards.

It is difficult to establish exactly when manufacture began. *The Autocar* reported in September 1896 that 'Mr Crowden (works manager) hopes to have his first British-built Bollée on the road this week'. Hopes are very far from being certainties, but by November *The Autocar* was able to report that nine Coventry Motettes were shown at the Stanley Cycle Show in London. The names Coventry Motette and Coventry Bollée were both applied to these vehicles, though Motette was generally adopted after manufacture passed out of Lawson's hands.

How many of these three-wheelers were made in 1896 is not certain, but even if there were no more than the nine seen at the Stanley Show one could claim that manufacture had started that year, which gives Humber the honour of being the first maker of series production cars in England, albeit they were three-wheelers and of foreign design. Manufacture lasted through to 1899. Some cars had side-by-side seating and were known as the Humber Motor Sociable. Motorcycles, tricycles and quadricycles were also made, and two-wheelers were built until 1930, having an excellent reputation for quality. Humber, with Sunbeam, were among the few firms to make bicycles, motorcycles and cars at the same time for a considerable period.

Various other experimental cars were made, including a mysterious vehicle, possibly electrically powered, built by C. H. Shacklock, manager of the Wolverhampton factory, in 1896. No details have survived, and there were no more four-wheeled Humbers until 1899, when a light two-seater called the Humber

Humber was never renowned as a commercial-vehicle maker, but from time to time delivery-van bodies were offered on car chassis. This is a 1905 Royal Humberette mail van.

A 1905 8/10 horsepower Coventry Humber tonneau. The tricar next to it might also be of Humber manufacture, but this is not certain.

Phaeton appeared. This had a front-mounted horizontal air-cooled engine with belt drive to the rear axle. Engine sizes of 3, 3½ and 5 horsepower were quoted, though it is not known if all were made. Experiments with these continued into 1900, when a curious machine called the MD Voiturette was built. This had front-wheel drive and rear-wheel steering and was started by lifting the steering wheel and giving it a sharp turn, which actuated a system of bevels, cross-shafts and chains. It is hardly surprising that this was never put into production, and for 1901 a more conventional Humber was built and was catalogued and priced at £275 standard, 300 guineas de luxe. It was powered by a 4½ horsepower De Dion Bouton engine, this make being used by Humber for their tricycles and quadricycles as well, and had shaft drive to the rear axle, with the unusual feature of two reverse speeds as well as two forward. The body was a rear-entrance tonneau, and a feature was the single-spoked steering wheel which was seen on all Humber cars until 1910.

In 1901 Humber acquired the services of Louis Hervé Coatalen (1880-1962), a French-born designer. (He went to Hillman in 1907 and later to Sunbeam, where he did his best-known work; all three British companies for which Coatalen worked ended up as parts of the Rootes Group.) Coatalen's early designs for Humber included 8 horsepower twin and 12 horsepower four-cylinder cars, followed in 1903 by a bigger four of 20 horsepower with a capacity of 5347 cc. This was a large car with seating for four or five passengers. With a gilled tube radiator and tonneau body, it cost 750 guineas, or with the more modern honeycomb radiator and Roi-des-Belges side entrance body, 800 guineas. A 9 horsepower three-cylinder car was also built, but it did not go into production.

The most important early Humber, and the car which established the company's reputation as a producer of four-wheelers, was the 5 horsepower (677 cc) single-cylinder Humberette, which was announced in June 1903. It had a vertical engine, two-speed transmission and shaft drive (no production Humber car was ever chain-driven), and it was the first model to be built at both the Coventry and the Beeston factories. The Beeston models were better finished, with such features as bucket seats and side doors. Prices were correspondingly higher, at £150 compared with £125 for the Coventry product. In the first six months Humberette production was 500 cars, of which 190 came from Beeston. In 1904 a larger-engined model, the 6½ horsepower (773 cc) Royal Humberette with three forward speeds, was introduced, also made in both factories. For such light cars the Humberettes were very reliable and good hill climbers. One owner, who had never handled a motor

car before, collected his machine from the factory and drove 321 miles (517 km) home without a hitch.

The popular little Humberettes were made to the end of the 1905 season, by which date the single-cylinder light car was out of date. Coatalen replaced it with a small four-cylinder 8/10 horsepower (1885 cc) car made at Coventry only. This was developed the following year into the 10/12 horsepower (2365 cc) which, with a larger 15 horsepower model, was the staple Coventry product for the next two years. Beeston turned out a considerably larger and more expensive product, the 16/20 and 30 horsepower cars of 3544 and 4942 cc respectively. In 1906 Beeston built fourteen examples of a large six-cylinder car

with engine rated at 30/40 horsepower and capacity of either 5652 or 6838 cc, according to different sources. The radiators were different from any other Humbers, being rounded in the manner of the Delaunay-Belleville or Hotchkiss. Beeston-built cars tended to be more up-market than those from Coventry; the 30 horsepower Beeston had four speeds and a gate change, while the 15 horsepower Coventry had only three speeds and the more old-fashioned quadrant change. The 10/12 horsepower from Coventry had a tubular frame, while all Beeston-built cars after the Humberette had pressed-steel channel-section frames. Bodies were mostly built in the factories and included two taxicab models, a two-passenger and a four-passenger, both on

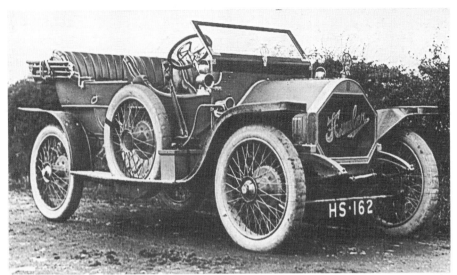

Above: *Described by 'The Autocar' as 'practically a Four Inch model', this is a sporting tourer with a 100 by 140 mm (4396 cc) engine. This was not a catalogued engine size, so it may well have come from a Four Inch racer. The gearbox had four forward speeds, and the lowest speed in top was only 4 mph (6 km/h).*

Below: *A two-seater powered by the 8 horsepower two-cylinder L-head engine introduced for 1909. This car can be seen at the National Motor Museum, Beaulieu.*

the 10/12 horsepower Coventry chassis. The latter had a shorter wheelbase as the driver was mounted over the engine in a forward-control position.

By 1906 Humber was one of the largest British makers of motor cars, with an output which reached 75 vehicles per week, 50 from Coventry and 25 from Beeston. Profits rose from £6500 in 1905 to £154,000 in 1907, yet the following year saw a loss of £23,000, due to a general slump in the motor industry because of over-production. It was decided to close the Beeston factory and to concentrate production on a new factory at Stoke on the outskirts of Coventry. New models were added at both ends of the range, an 8 horsepower two-cylinder car of 1527 cc and a 30 horsepower six of 5589 cc, the first six-cylinder Humber to be made in any numbers. From 1910 the cars were gradually modernised, receiving detachable wheels in that year, with the option of wire instead of wood. Cylinders were pair-cast from 1910, with the first monobloc four being the 1744 cc 11 horsepower of 1911. This also intro-

duced L-head engines, with a single cam shaft in place of the two camshafts on either side of the block of the older T-head layout. By 1914 the only T-head model was the big 4849 cc 28 horsepower four.

Between 1912 and 1915 there was a boom in cyclecars, very light vehicles using engines and other components from motorcycles. Many of the cheapest ones were crude and unsatisfactory, and Humber wisely avoided these. Instead they brought out a shaft-driven light car powered by a 998 cc air-cooled V-twin engine. The dimensions (84 by 90 mm, 3.3 by 3.5 inches) were the same as those of the single-cylinder Humber motorcycle, though Humber never made a V-twin motorcycle as large as this. The name Humberette was revived for this light car, which had a tubular chassis, three-speed quadrant gearbox and non-detachable wheels. With screen, hood, horn and three lights, it sold for £125. A water-cooled model was available for 1914 at £135, and for 1915 water cooling was standard. The Humberette was

A 28 horsepower limousine, c.1911. With a 4849 cc engine, this was the largest Humber made between 1910 and 1914. Note the speaking tube by the chauffeur's ear, enabling him to receive instructions from the passengers behind the glass screen.

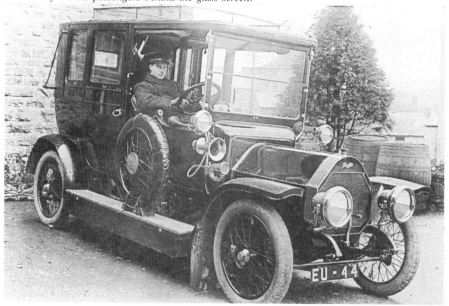

A popular model of the period immediately before the First World War, the 1914 11 horsepower still used Humber-made wire wheels, whereas the newly introduced 10 and 14 horsepower cars had artillery wheels.

appreciably cheaper than other Humbers, which started at £255 for a 10 horsepower two-seater.

Between 1909 and 1914 Humber production ran at about two thousand cars per year, reaching 2500 in 1914. This put the company in third position among British manufacturers, after Ford and Wolseley. Car production was suspended in 1916, but motorcycles were made throughout the First World War. As early as 1909 Humber had opened an aircraft department, making fifty Bleriot-type monoplanes, followed by a number of Humber Sommer pusher biplanes. All these were powered by Humber three- or four-cylinder engines. In 1910 the world's first airmail service was operated in India, using Humber aeroplanes. The Aero Department closed in 1911, but the experience gained was of great help during the war, when the company built BR-2 engines designed by W. O. Bentley, and also complete Avro 504 aircraft.

The Humberette weighed less than 350 kg (7 cwt) so was classed as a cyclecar, though it was better built than most of that type. This is a 1913 model with air-cooled engine.

Above: *The Beeston Humber which won the Heavy Touring Car class in the 1907 Tourist Trophy. Its driver, George Mills, had been a celebrated competitor on Humber bicycles. Note the large screen intended to simulate the drag imposed by closed coachwork.*

Below: *The racing car entered in the 1908 Tourist Trophy by the Coventry factory. Driven by its designer, G. W. A. Brown, it crashed in practice and retired on the sixth lap of the race.*

The mysterious 60 horsepower six-cylinder Beeston Humber with Delaunay-Belleville-like radiator which competed for the 'Graphic' Trophy in the Isle of Man in 1906. It was the only Humber to be chain-driven. On the left is Glentworth's 50 horsepower Napier.

HUMBER IN COMPETITION

Humber is not thought of as a sporting make, but up to 1914 it took part in a variety of competitions with a considerable degree of success. A 20 horsepower car driven by J. W. Cross defeated several Daimlers in the Irish Fortnight of competitions that followed the 1903 Gordon Bennett Race. They took part in many road trials (forerunners of today's rallies). Humbers were most active in the Tourist Trophy races held in the Isle of Man between 1905 and 1908, and again in 1914. The early events were for touring cars with road equipment, and in 1905 two 16/20 horsepower Humbers were entered. They were not particularly successful, but in 1906 the designers Coatalen and Pullinger each drove a car,

Coatalen a 20 horsepower Coventry-built model and Pullinger a 16/20 horsepower Beeston-built car. Pullinger finished fifth, with his team mate in sixth place. Coatalen's car bore no relation to the 10/12 horsepower Coventry product but was closer to the 15 horsepower brought out the following year, so the company was already following the practice of using racing to test a future production car. In *The Graphic* Trophy race which followed the 1906 TT there appeared a mysterious Beeston Humber described as a 60 horsepower six-cylinder car. It had the Delaunay-like round radiator of the 30/40 horsepower cars and possibly used the same engine, but it was unusual in being the only Humber to have chain drive.

Above: *The Humber team in the 1908 Two Thousand Miles Trial, seen at Brooklands. (Left to right) 30 horsepower and 20 horsepower Beeston, 15 and 10/12 horsepower Coventry cars. The Beestons were the only two cars from any company to achieve completely non-stop runs.*

The 1907 TT had two classes, for standard touring cars and for heavy touring cars, which had to carry screens to simulate the drag imposed by landaulette coachwork. Four Humbers were entered, two in each class, and all with different-sized engines. Jimmy Reid's 4½ litre Beeston car was second in the standard class, while George Mills won the heavy class with a 7.2 litre car, also from Beeston. Very different cars con-

tested the 1908 TT, for the regulations stipulated a maximum weight of 1600 pounds (726 kg) and a cylinder bore limit of 4 inches (10 cm) — hence the event's popular name, the Four Inch Race. This meant that all competing companies had to design special sporting models. Two of Humber's entries came from Beeston and had single overhead-camshaft engines with radiators mounted behind, and a wire-mesh cage over them, while

The only survivor of the Burgess-designed twin-overhead-cam 1914 TT cars, this car regularly competes in vintage racing today. It is seen here at Silverstone in 1962, driven by Kenneth Neve, who still owns it.

the 'body' was confined to two bucket seats ahead of a bolster fuel tank, with neither doors nor windscreen. Neither finished the race, nor did a more conventional-looking car from Coventry driven by its designer, G. W. A. Brown.

No further Tourist Trophy races were held until 1914, when there was a two-day event over 600 miles (966 km). Cars were limited by weight (minimum 2300 pounds, 1043 kg) and capacity (maximum 3310 cc), and most entries were racing cars of Grand Prix type. Humber had no such car to pattern their TT entries on, but F. T. Burgess designed a car which was closely based on the Grand Prix Peugeot, having twin overhead-camshaft engines with four valves per cylinder, a capacity of 3295 cc and output of 100 brake horsepower. All three cars retired in the race, though they had some success at Brooklands after the war, and one still competes in vintage events up to the present day.

Humber had numerous successes in sprints, hill climbs and reliability trials in the pre-1914 era, and W. G. Tuck established several records at Brooklands in a streamlined single-seater fitted with either an 11.9 or a 14 horsepower engine.

A sporting two-seater, probably a 10 horsepower, competing in the Caerphilly Hill Climb in 1914.

Above: *A four-seater saloon body on a 1922 11.4 horsepower chassis. Closed coachwork was still in the minority; not until 1926 did it outnumber open bodies on British-built cars.*

Below: *Two/three-seater 'chummy' body on the 1923 8 horsepower chassis. This was renamed 8/18 for 1925 and was enlarged to the 9/20 for 1926.*

Still essentially a pre-First World War design, this is a 1922 15.9 horsepower, which was descended from the 1914 14 horsepower model.

THE VINTAGE HUMBERS

The history of Humber in the 1920s was aptly summed up by the authors of *The Humber Story* as 'established conservatism'. The company was fortunate in getting back into production within a few months of the Armistice, and they were not going to waste time trying out new models. The pre-war range of six models (including the Humberette) was whittled down to two, the 1593 cc 10 horsepower and the 2474 cc 14 horsepower. Both were similar to 1914 specification, which was quite modern for the time, with monobloc four-cylinder engines (detachable head on the 10 horsepower), unit construction with a four-speed gearbox, and electric lighting and starting. These two were continued until 1923 with little change apart from increases in engine capacity to 1743 and 2815 cc, the names being changed to 11.4 and 15.9 horsepower.

For the 1923 season Humber made their most radical innovations of the decade, with a range of inlet-over-exhaust valve engines in place of the old side-valvers. These were applied to the existing models, which were joined by a new small car, the 985 cc 8 horsepower. With a wheelbase of 7 feet 10½ inches (240 cm), this was not much larger than the contemporary Austin Seven, though it was higher-priced and made in much smaller numbers. For a small car of its day it was very well equipped with five lamps, good instrumentation and weather protection. Bodies included a three-seater saloon. Prices were £250 for the 'chummy' open two/three-seater, and £310 for the saloon. A total of 2400 8 horsepowers were made, of which only 277 were saloons.

For 1925 Humber adopted the fashion for giving two horsepowers in their designations, the Royal Automobile Club rating and the approximate developed brake horsepower. Thus the 8 became the 8/18, the 11.4 was bored out and became the 12/25, and the 15.9 became the 15/40. An innovation of 1925, seen only as an option on the 15/40, was that of front-wheel brakes. They were standardised on the 1926 15/40 and reached the smallest of the range in February 1927. Two new models appeared in 1926, the six-cylinder 20/55 of 3016 cc, Humber's first six since 1909, and a four-cylinder derivative with the same cylinder dimensions, the 2050 cc 14/40. The 20/55 was the start of a long line of larger Humbers which was continued in the Snipe, Super Snipe and Pullman. For the first time since the war, a limousine and landaulette with chauffeur's division were offered, bringing Humber back into the carriage trade. As the authors of *The Humber Story* said, they sold well to

Above: With the arrival of the 9/20, full four-seater coachwork was possible for the first time on the smallest Humber chassis. It is seen coming through one of Coventry's old gateways.

Below: A 1927 20/55 saloon, the first of a long line of large Humbers which was continued in the Snipes and Pullmans. This saloon cost £940. A landaulette was the same price, and a tourer £725.

Above: *A Weymann fabric coupé on a 1929 16/50 horsepower chassis. Fabric bodies were offered on all Humbers from 1928 to 1932.*

Below: *A very handsome drophead coupé on the 1929 20/65 horsepower chassis. The non-standard disc wheels give it a Daimler look.*

those who aspired to own a Rolls-Royce but could not afford one.

Humbers remained conservative in the late 1920s, though steady improvements were made. Low-pressure tyres were used from 1927, and front-wheel brakes were standardised, while body lines were gradually improved. In 1928 fabric-bodied saloons were offered throughout the range. Wire wheels were optional on all models from 1929, apart from the 14/40. Power was gradually increased, so that the 8/18 became the 9/20 and then the 9/28, and the 20/55 became the 20/65. A new smaller six was the 2110 cc 16/50, and for 1930 this was joined by what was to become one of Humber's best known cars, the Snipe. This had the same chassis as the 16/50 and shared the same body styles, but under the bonnet was a 3498 cc six-cylinder engine which developed 72 brake horsepower and gave the Snipe a top speed of 75 mph (120 km/h), so long as the coachwork was not too heavy. For those who preferred dignified luxury to speed there was a long-wheelbase model for formal coachwork called the Pullman. Like Snipe, this was a name which would remain in Humber's catalogues for a long time. The 16/50 was continued, being distinguishable from its larger sister only by its lack of radiator shutters and Snipe mascot. Prices were £70 lower for all body styles.

The 9/28 was dropped after the 1930 season, and only 99 were made that year, out of a total of 1248. Overall, it was Humber's best year before the Rootes take-over, with 5618 cars delivered.

The 1931 four-light saloon was one of seven body styles on the Snipe and cost £515.

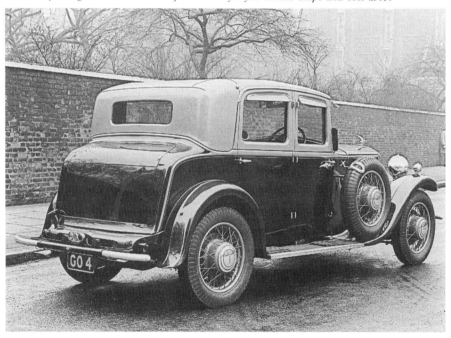

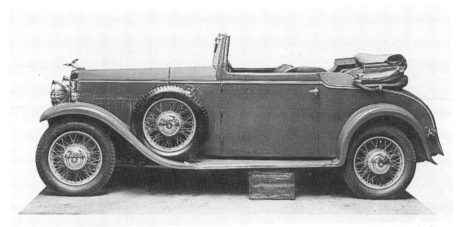

Though Humber offered a wide range of coachwork, some bodies were also made by outside firms. This is a drophead by Offord on a 1932 Snipe. The Snipe mascot and bonnet louvres were the only external signs that distinguished a Snipe from the smaller-engined 16/50.

ROOTES MOTORS TAKES OVER

The growth of the Rootes Group was one of the major success stories of the inter-war years. William Rootes had started a small engineering business in the Kent village of Hawkhurst in 1898, later becoming an important dealer in Maidstone. His sons, William and Reginald, joined him in the 1920s and the company moved into prestigious headquarters in Devonshire House, Piccadilly, London, in 1926. In the same year they bought the coachbuilders Thrupp and Maberly, established in 1760, and soon afterwards they began buying Humber shares, with a view to gaining control and becoming manufacturers as well as retailers. By 1931 they held 60 per cent of the shares and took over control in July 1932. This meant that they owned two car makers, Hillman and Humber, and the commercial vehicle firm Commer Cars, which Humber had bought in 1925.

Although the Rootes acquisition was eventually to lead to badge engineering within the group, there was little sign of it to start with, as far as Humber was concerned. The 9/28 had been discontinued at the end of 1930, and the 16/50 and Snipe were continued for 1933 little changed in appearance, though with new side-valve engines in place of the traditional overhead-inlet-valve units. The smaller engine was enlarged from 2110 to 2276 cc, for which the car was renamed the 16/60. The 3498 cc Snipe unit gave an extra 5 brake horsepower, at 78 brake horsepower. Frames were now cruciform-braced, and engines were rubber-mounted ('cushioned power'), the latter a feature shared with Hillman. The same bodies were offered, with the addition of an attractive four-light sports saloon peculiar to the Snipe, with dual-tone paintwork and unusual side windows curved at their lower edges. The long-wheelbase Pullman was also continued, the 132 inch (335 cm) wheelbase remaining unchanged until 1948.

A new Humber for 1933, which slotted into the Rootes range between the Hillman Minx and the Humber 16/60, was the Twelve. This was essentially a scaled-down Snipe, with 1669 cc 42 brake horsepower four-cylinder engine, cruciform frame and Bendix brakes. The saloon body was an undistinguished six-light affair not unlike that of the Minx, though at 98¼ inches (250 cm), the Humber's wheelbase was 6¼ inches (16 cm) longer. It also had a four-speed gearbox, which

19

Above: *By 1934 the open tourer was a relatively rare bodystyle, but this was still available on the Snipe chassis. It was not offered in 1935 or later.*

Left: *The Twelve sports tourer which Lionel Martin (here in the passenger seat) drove in the 1933 Alpine Rally.*

Below: *The Vogue pillarless saloon said to have been designed by the couturier Captain Molyneux, on a 1934 Twelve chassis.*

1937 was the last year for the Twelve; the forward position of the engine made for a less good-looking car, though a bonus for the driver was the all-synchromesh gearbox from the Hillman Minx.

the Minx would not receive until 1934. It was not a particularly imposing car, though one was used by the Mayor of Launceston, Tasmania, as official transport for several years. More interesting coachwork was also seen on the Twelve, including a sports tourer with cut-away doors, which Lionel Martin drove in the Alpine Rally, and the Vogue, a two-door saloon with pillarless side windows and plunging belt line. This was said to have been designed by the couturier Captain Molyneux, and like the Snipe sports saloon it came in dual colours. With disc wheels, it was a handsome little car, described by the late Michael Sedgwick as 'perfect for the well-heeled housewife' at £335. It lost some of its attraction in 1935, when engines were moved forward and the radiator grille was given a pronounced backward slope. A bonus, however, was the Hillman Minx's all-synchromesh gearbox. The Twelve was made until 1937, a total of 8486 being made.

The 16/60 and Snipe received the sloping grille for 1934, when synchromesh arrived, though not on all speeds as with the Twelve. Other features of these cars were built-in jacks, automatic choke and free wheels, while for 1935 there was the option of Laycock de Normanville semi-automatic transmission. This used a steering-column lever operating in a small quadrant and was similar to the

Wilson preselector, except that one could not preselect the gear, the change being immediate on moving the lever. The journalist Dudley Noble took a de Normanville-equipped Snipe towing a caravan through the Sahara, covering several thousand miles of near-roadless conditions without trouble. The de Normanville gearbox lasted for only two seasons though, because of difficulty of manufacture and because most customers were perfectly happy with synchromesh.

The big Humbers were completely redesigned for 1936, with larger engines of 4086 cc, transverse-leaf independent front suspension and more streamlined bodies. The suspension was the work of the American designer Barney Roos, who had used a similar system for his previous employers, Studebaker. After a short time with Humber he moved back to the United States and to Willys Overland, where he was responsible for improvements to the engine which went into the Jeep. The new Humbers were available in a wide price range, from £445 for a 2.7 litre Eighteen to £975 for a Pullman *sedanca de ville*. This was a rare body style by the late 1930s, with open front compartment for the chauffeur, and when they were seen it was more likely to be on Rolls-Royce or Daimler chassis. The Pullman limousine was a more popular style and offered elegant, luxurious

A Pullman landaulette used by the Duke and Duchess of York (later King George VI and Queen Elizabeth) during their visit to Edinburgh in 1935. Humbers were popular with the Royal Family for tours and visits both at home and abroad.

and reasonably fast motoring for only £735. Pullman bodies were by Rootes's own coachbuilder, Thrupp and Maberly. The Snipe was aimed at export markets as well as home sales, and Dudley Noble was dispatched on several continental trips, including eight days in Swiss ski-ing resorts (when driving to such places was thought very adventurous by Britons), ten capitals in ten days, and a trip to the little visited regions of Yugoslavia, Bulgaria and Turkey. Rootes hoped for Empire sales as well, but the average farmer or district commissioner in Africa preferred to buy American cars.

During the last few years before the Second World War badge engineering crept into the Humber range. For 1938 the Snipe name was given to a saloon which shared a body and wheelbase with the Hillman Fourteen, though engines were larger and still Humber-designed; the Snipe used a 3183 cc six, while the same car with a 2576 cc engine was called the Sixteen. The previous Snipe with

A Snipe saloon which took part in the 1937 Welsh Rally.

4086 cc was renamed the Snipe Imperial and for 1938 was offered with a new razor-edged four-light sports-saloon body, as well as a six-light saloon and drophead coupé. 1939 Snipe Imperials had hydraulic brakes, as did the smaller Sixteen and Snipe. The Pullman, despite its weight, did not receive hydraulics until the 1940 season, by which time hardly any were being made for the civilian market, though military top brass rode in them.

A new model for 1939, which had a better performance than any pre-war Humber, was the Super Snipe. This followed the popular formula of a large engine in a smaller chassis, in this case the 100 brake horsepower 4086 cc six in the 114 inch (290 cm) wheelbase of the Sixteen/Snipe. The most popular body was the four-light razor-edge sports saloon also seen on the Snipe Imperial, though it could be had as a saloon or a drophead coupé too. Top speed was 85 mph (137 km/h) and it could reach 50 mph (80 km/h) in 11.6 seconds, but it was slower than a Ford V8 (87 mph, 140 km/h), which cost only £280 compared with the Super Snipe's £385. Nevertheless there were enough customers who valued the Humber's quality and rather looked down on American cars, and the Super Snipe sold about 1500 examples in the 1938-9 season. 1940 models had larger luggage boots, though only a few were made.

One of the Thrupp and Maberly-bodied Super Snipe open staff cars, similar to those used by Field Marshal Montgomery. The large-section tyres also featured on military Super Snipe saloons.

HUMBER AT WAR

Humber was one of the major producers of military vehicles during the Second World War, and although they made aero-engines as well (in the Rootes Number 1 Shadow Factory near Coventry) four-wheeled vehicles formed the bulk of their production. The Super Snipe was one of the best known of the larger staff cars, along with its pre-war rival, the Ford V8. The military version differed from the civilian design in a number of ways. The most obvious was that the rear of the body was cut away so that the wings would clear the ground even when the car was climbing a steep gradient. The springs were set up to give greater ground clearance, and the track was increased as well. Larger tyres were used, being 9.00 by 13 Dunlop Traks with a pressure of only 20 pounds per square inch.

Most Super Snipe staff cars were saloons or estate cars, but open tourers were also made for desert work, coachwork being Thrupp and Maberly. The most famous of these was 'Old Faithful', a 1941 model which served Field Marshal Montgomery in the Eighth Army throughout his North African campaign from El Alamein onwards, and in Italy as far as the river Sangro. He later used another similar car, but 'Old Faithful' still exists and can be seen at the Museum of Army Transport at Beverley. A small number of Super Snipes were fitted with saloon bodies in Germany by Karmann of Osnabruck, for use by the British occupying forces. These originated as 8 cwt (406 kg) trucks known as FFWs (Fitted For Wireless). At the end of the war they were no longer needed for this work, but there was a serious shortage of staff transport, so it seemed logical to take advantage of skilled coachbuilders on the spot. Karmann, which had been founded in 1874, later made the famous

Karmann-Ghia coupés on the Volkswagen Beetle chassis and today produces the convertible versions of the Volkswagen Golf.

Humber also made some 3600 light armoured cars (Ironsides), of which a few were luxuriously fitted out by Thrupp and Maberly for use by the Royal Family and cabinet ministers. They were known as 'Special Ironside Saloons'. Other contributions to the war effort were 4300 rear-engined four-wheel-drive scout cars and 6500 four-wheel-drive Heavy Utilities. This was a remarkable vehicle, being the only 4 × 4 machine of its type made in Britain at the time. In concept it was an ancestor of the four-door Range Rover and Toyota Land Cruiser type of vehicle, which did not become common until the 1970s. It was intended to transport staff officers at high speed (maximum 63 mph, 101 km/h) over good roads, and also to keep going where roads were non-existent, on sand or deep mud. Although purpose-built for military needs, the Heavy Utility used many components from civilian vehicles, including the 4 litre engine and transverse-leaf front suspension. The Snipe's four-speed gearbox was also used, drive passing via Layrub jackshaft to a transfer box, from the base of which universally jointed shafts ran to front and rear axles. The transfer box enabled the car to operate in two-wheel drive on metalled roads, and to switch to four-wheel drive on a lower set of ratios for cross-country work. To change to four-wheel drive, all that was necessary was to double-declutch, increase engine speed and pull the transfer lever upwards. Its cross-country performance seemed astonishing to *The Autocar* in 1943, when four-wheel-drive cars were virtually unknown, apart from the much smaller Jeep. A loose-surface gradient of 1 in 2.5 was climbed with ease.

Variants on the Humber 4 × 4 included a general staff officer's version with more comfortable interior, map-reading lamp and a sliding roof, and a 'cross-country saloon' with car-type boot, bodied by Thrupp and Maberly. The cars were widely used in the North African campaign and on the Western Front, and also by the RAF Mountain Rescue Service, which was formed in North Wales in 1942. Production ended in 1945. *The Autocar* observed that 'it was the kind of car to have a strong appeal after the war to farmers or to large estates'. Unfortunately the Rootes brothers did not make a civilian version, leaving it to Rover to take up the challenge, though the early Land-Rovers were much more spartan and cramped than Humbers.

The 4 × 4 Heavy Utility was an ancestor of today's Range Rover type of vehicle with comfortable seating for seven and a good off-road performance. The body was made of steel and wood and had a divided panel at the back; the upper part with two small windows could be swung open, and the lower part let down as a tailboard.

The 1946 Hawk was really a pre-war Hillman Fourteen with hydraulic brakes, but a Humber radiator grille and disc wheels gave it a distinguished appearance, and it was hard to tell it from a Super Snipe. Top speed, though, was only 65 mph (105 km/h), against the Super Snipe's 80 mph plus (130 km/h).

HUMBER IN THE POST-WAR YEARS

Like most other manufacturers, Humber based their post-war range on the cars they had been making in 1939. The smallest model, the Hawk, was a 1944 cc four-cylinder Hillman Fourteen with Humber radiator grille, hydraulic brakes and *de luxe* trim. The same body was used for the Snipe and Super Snipe, which used pre-war six-cylinder engines of 2731 and 4086 cc respectively. The Super Snipe was widely used by Britain's police forces. Only the one six-light saloon body was available. At the top of the range was the Pullman limousine, similar to the model used by the Army. A very small number of *sedanca de villes* were also made on this chassis, bodied by H. J. Mulliner.

The Hawk Mark I became the Mark II in 1947 when it received steering-column gearchange, and it was considerably modified in the Mark III for 1949, which had a new four-light body, headlamps faired into the wings, curved windscreen and coil independent front suspension in place of the transverse leaves. The engine was the same 1944 cc four, said by Michael Sedgwick to guarantee nil performance — actually 72 mph (116 km/h) and 0-50 mph (80 km/h) in 21.2 seconds.

The Snipe was dropped from the 1949 range, and the Super Snipe and Pullman were less radically restyled than the Hawk, receiving wing-mounted headlamps and a smaller vertical grille. All Humbers now had column change (with full synchromesh from 1951) but the bigger cars retained the old suspension. A small number of handsome drophead coupés were built by Tickford on the Super Snipe chassis, and the Pullman was available as a seven-passenger saloon without division under the name Imperial.

Humbers sold well in the early post-war years, some 13,200 finding customers in 1951, of which 8000 were Hawks, 4400 Super Snipes and 800 Pullman/Imperials. The Hawk received a bigger engine of 2267 cc that year, and in 1954 overhead valves were at last introduced, on a detuned version of the Sunbeam 90 engine. The previous year the Super Snipe also had overhead valves in a slightly larger engine of 4138 cc, which gave 116 brake horsepower and a top speed of 91 mph (146 km/h). Overdrive was available on this Super Snipe Mark IV from 1955, and an optional automatic transmission for 1956. The body was now

Above and below: *Two generations of the post-war Pullman, a 1947 limousine with pre-war styling, and a 1953 Imperial seven-seater saloon, which had steering-column change for the all-synchromesh gearbox.*

Top and centre: *Mark II and Mark III versions of the Super Snipe, made from 1949-50 and 1951-2 respectively. There was little difference between the two, but the rear wheel spats and larger overriders gave the later car a heavier appearance. The Mark II illustrated provided official transport for Sir Alexander Coutanche, Bailiff of Jersey, who is standing next to the car.*

Right: *A Mark III Super Snipe during the 1952 Eastbourne Rally. The model's best success was Maurice Gatsonides' second place in the 1950 Monte Carlo Rally.*

The 1954 Hawk Mark VI had a 2267 cc overhead-valve engine which was a detuned version of that used in the Sunbeam 90.

a four-light saloon in similar style to that of the Hawk. The Pullman and Imperial also received the new engine for 1953/4, but few were made, and these large and impressive cars were dropped from the range after 1954.

A new Hawk appeared for 1957 for which the numbering system was started all over again, so that whereas the 1956 model was the Mark VI, the new car was the Mark I. It had an American-style all-enveloping saloon body with wrap-around windscreen and rear window, unitary construction and the option of automatic transmission. The engine was the 2267 cc four from the previous Hawk. Front disc brakes were offered on the 1961 Mark II, while the Mark III (mid 1962) had minor styling changes and dual overdrive option. The last of the Hawks, the Mark IV of 1965-7, had more angular styling, a rear anti-roll bar and, like the bigger cars, synchromesh on all forward speeds. In 1959 the Super Snipe was given the same unitary body as the Hawk and a 2655 cc six-cylinder engine. Most were saloons, but alternative bodies (also available on the Hawk) were a touring limousine with division and an estate car. A larger engine of 2965 cc came in 1960

The Super Snipe Mark IV (1953-6) was the first Humber to have all-overhead valves, and it also featured an all-synchromesh gearbox, overdrive from 1955, and the option of automatic transmission from 1956.

*The new Hawk intro-
duced for 1957 had a
completely new integral
construction body,
though the old 2267 cc
engine was still used. It
was photographed on
the Otto Beit Bridge
crossing the Zambesi be-
tween what were then
Northern and Southern
Rhodesia.*

Above: *The estate-car version of the 1958 Hawk.*

Below: *For 1959 the Super Snipe received the same body as the Hawk, though distinguished by a more ornate grille. Under the bonnet was a 2655 cc six cylinder overhead-valve engine with square dimensions (82.55 by 82.55 mm).*

Above: *The Series II Super Snipe of 1960 had a larger engine of 2965 cc, now over-square, and the Series III, seen here, was the first British car to have quad headlights.*

Centre: *In 1965 the name Imperial was revived for the luxury version of the Super Snipe, which featured a black leatherette roof covering and cost £284 more. A four-speed synchromesh gearbox was available, but nearly all Imperials were sold with automatic transmissions.*
Below: *The Sceptre Mark II of 1965-7 was no more than a Hillman Super Minx with a different radiator grille, sharing the Hillman's front disc brakes and optional automatic transmission.*

The last car to bear the Humber name was another Sceptre, this time a Hillman Hunter with twin-carburettor engine and quad headlamps. New for 1968, it was made with little change until 1976.

(Series II), and the 1963 Series III had a redesigned radiator grille and four head-lamps, the first British car to do so. The name Imperial was revived for the last of the Super Snipe family, this being dis-tinguished from lesser cars by its black leatherette roof covering. It cost £284 more than the Super Snipe, nearly all having automatic transmission, though a four-speed synchromesh box was avail-able.

The Rootes Group was acquired by Chrysler in 1967, and the Humbers were dropped in favour of the Australian-built Chrysler Valiant, though hardly any of these were sold in Britain. The French-built 180 might have carried the Humber name, but this was considered to be in-sufficiently well known internationally and so it was called a Chrysler 180. There was a smaller Humber, the Sceptre, which had been introduced in 1963. This was a typical piece of badge engineering, having Hillman Super Minx body, Sun-beam Rapier radiator grille and Humber Super Snipe's quad headlamps. The engine was shared with the Super Minx,

a 1592 cc four enlarged to 1725 cc in 1966. Two years later the Sceptre name went on to an even less individual car; this was a Hillman Hunter with twin car-burettors (as used in the Sunbeam Rapier) and quad headlamps, made from 1968 to 1976. It had better trim, includ-ing items such as a wood fascia, and at £1139 cost £277 more than the Hunter. By its demise in 1976, the Sceptre had gone up to £2614 for a saloon, and £2851 for the estate car, which was available only for the last two seasons.

Thus, like many great British marques, Humber went out of existence with a mundane car, but it was mourned by countless motorists with memories of Snipes and Super Snipes and by vintage enthusiasts who still cherished their 8/18s and 14/40s. The later Humbers were made in Rootes's Ryton-on-Dunsmore factory, while the old Stoke works were used for making engines for the whole group, and later for preparation of the Hunter kits which went to Iran, where they were assembled and sold under the name Peykan.

31

FURTHER READING

Only one book, apart from this one, is exclusively devoted to Humber cars:

Demaus, A. B., and Tarring, J. C. *The Humber Story, 1898-1932*. Alan Sutton, 1989.

Among other titles which refer to Humber are:

Baldwin, Nick (editor). *The World Guide to Automobiles*. McDonald Orbis, 1987.
Georgano, G. N. (editor). *The Complete Encyclopedia of Motorcars*. Ebury Press, 1982.
Nicholson, T. R. *The Vintage Car, 1919-1930*. B. T. Batsford, 1966.
Sedgwick, Michael. *Cars of the 1930s*. B. T. Batsford, 1970.
Sedgwick, Michael. *The Motor Car, 1945-1956*. B. T. Batsford, 1979.
Sedgwick, Michael, and Gillies, Mark. *A-Z of Cars of the 1930s*. Bay View Books, 1989.
Sedgwick, Michael, and Gillies, Mark. *A-Z of Cars, 1945-1970*. Temple Press, 1986.

PLACES TO VISIT

Humber cars can be seen in a number of museums, including the following:

Bicton Park (James Countryside Collection), East Budleigh, Budleigh Salterton, Devon EX9 7DP. Telephone: 0395 68465. 1925 car.
C. M. Booth Collection of Historic Vehicles, 63-7 High Street, Rolvenden, Cranbrook, Kent TN17 4LP. Telephone: 0580 241234. 1905 Humber Olympia Tricar.
Museum of Army Transport, Flemingate, Beverley, North Humberside HU17 0NG. Telephone 0482 860445. 1941 Super Snipe staff car, 'Old Faithful', used by Field Marshal Montgomery.
Museum of British Road Transport, St Agnes Lane, Hale Street, Coventry, West Midlands CV1 1PN. Telephone: 0203 832425. This collection includes several Humber motorcycles and tricycles and an 1897 Coventry Motette, as well as several cars.
Myreton Motor Museum, Aberlady, Longniddry, East Lothian EH32 0PZ. Telephone: 08757 288. 1926 15/40, 1929 9/28, 1936 Snipe, 1903 2¾ horsepower motorcycle.
National Motor Museum, John Montagu Building, Beaulieu, Brockenhurst, Hampshire SO4 7ZN. Telephone: 0590 612345. 1909 8 horsepower two-cylinder.

CLUBS
There are two clubs devoted to Humber vehicles which hold regular rallies and offer advice to owners and would-be owners:

The Humber Register. Secretary: H. Gregory, 176 London Road, St Albans, Hertfordshire.
The Post-Vintage Humber Car Club. Secretary: Neil Gibbins, 2 Melton Court, Havelock Road, Croydon, Surrey CR0 6QQ.